Prayer Shawl Reflections

> **"** Let this be written for a future generation, that a people not yet created may praise the Lord. **"** —Psalm 102:18

These devotions that God has given to me to write down are my legacy to pass on to fellow believers in this generation and in the generations to come. My prayer is the words of Psalm 19:14, *"May the words of my mouth and the meditation of my heart be pleasing in your sight, O Lord, my Rock and my Redeemer."* Writing these devotions made me dig deeper into God's word and not just look at the face value of the text. I challenge each of you to dig into God's word and claim the precious promises that are there for each of us.

The title "Prayer Shawl Reflections" comes from Proverbs 27:19 "As water reflects a face, so a man's heart reflects the man." We pray for our shawls to be a reflection of Jesus' love and caring that reflects on to the receivers of the shawl. "And we, who with unveiled faces all reflect the Lord's glory, are being transformed into His likeness with ever-increasing glory, which comes from the Lord, who is the Spirit." May we all strive to reflect our Lord's love and caring on those around us.

Prayer Shawl Reflections

ISBN: 978-1-60920-048-0

Printed in the United States of America

©2012 by Karen Doolaard

Cover design by Ajoyin Publishing, Inc.

Interior design by Ajoyin Publishing, Inc.

Library of Congress Cataloging-in-Publication Data

API

Ajoyin Publishing, Inc.

P.O. 342

Three Rivers, MI 49093

www.ajoyin.com

Please direct your inquiries to admin@ajoyin.com

Prayer Shawl Reflections

Devotions for those receiving prayer shawls

by

Karen Doolaard

Ajoyin Publishing, Inc.

PO Box 342

Three Rivers, MI 49093

1.888.273.4JOY

www.ajoyin.com

ACKNOWLEDGMENTS

Many thanks:

to Sherma, my fellow born-in-South-Dakota-living-in-Michigan friend. Her insight and suggestions are so helpful and encouraging.

to Bev – my fellow pool pal who checks my spelling, sentence structure and is so willing to encourage me on my journey. God has truly given you the gift of encouragement and you are so willing to share that with others.

to God for giving me these words to write down, for His gift of His Son and eternal life. We can anticipate a wonderful reunion in heaven with our Lord.

CONTENTS

CONTENTS

1 Contentment

5 Be Still

9 Caregivers

13 Heavenly Minded

17 No More Tears

21 Pet Power

25 Praying for Me

29 He Knows My Name

33 I Can Do All Things

37 Meat and Potatoes

41 Breathless Babies

45 Infertility

49 Single

53 Loss Through Death

57 Single Again

61 Chronic Pain

65 Depression

69 Songs in the Night

73 One Step Closer to Heaven

77 No Worries, Mate!

81 Aged to Perfection

85 Hands to Work, Hearts to God

89 Crossing Jordan

93 Parachute Blanket

97 Freely Given

101 Alzeimers

105 Special Needs Person

109 Disaster

113 Let Your Light Shine

117 Great Joy

CONTENTMENT

" I have learned the secret of being content in any and every situation, whether well fed or hungry, whether living in plenty or in want."

—Philippians 4:20

God is there in the situation you are in. Whether it be physical illness, emotional hurting or spiritual struggles, God is there. Knowing God is with us gives us contentment in our situation. Jesus experienced physical pain, emotional hurting and spiritual struggles during His ministry here on earth.

We don't understand why these things are happening to you but rest assured, God is in control! Matthew 10:29 tells us, *"Are not two sparrows sold for a penny? Yet not one of them will fall to the ground apart from the will of your Father."* Then in verse 31 it goes on with, *"So don't be afraid; you are worth more than many sparrows."* It is our choice to become bitter or better through this situation.

Helen Keller said, "The marvelous richness of human experience would lose something of rewarding joy if there were no limitations to overcome. The hilltop hour would not be half so wonderful if there were no dark valleys to traverse."

1

Draw close to God, rest in Him! Surround yourself with fellow Christians who are praying for you, let God's word speak to you, sing His praises in the dark hours of the night. Humans cannot always travel this road with you, but God is there with you every step of the way.

The prayer shawl that was given to you is a tangible thing that you can wrap around you and feel the prayers of God's people for you as well as Jesus' arms around you. It can physically warm you as well as spiritually uplift you.

.

REFLECTIONS

"

"

REFLECTIONS

"

„

BE STILL

" Be still, and know that I am God. "
—Psalm 46:10

I needed the quiet, so He took me aside,
Into the shadows where we could confide;

Away from the bustle where all the day long
I hurried and worried, when active and strong.

I needed the quiet, though at first I rebelled,
But gently, so gently, my cross He upheld,

And whispered so sweetly of spiritual things,
Though weakened in body, my spirit took wings.

To heights never dreamed of when active and gay,
He loved me so gently, He drew me away.

I needed the quiet, no prison my bed –
But a beautiful valley of blessing instead,

A place to grow richer, in Jesus to hide,
I needed the quiet, so He drew me aside.
                    —Alice H. Mortenson

It takes a lot to get our attention sometimes! Our lives are so busy in whatever stage of life we are in. Retired people talk about being busier than they have ever been in their lives. It takes a conscious effort to back away and just be still. Sometimes God uses physical illness to slow us down so He can get our attention.

As Elijah found out in I Kings 19:11–13, God is not necessarily in the big, noisy things. God sent the wind, earthquake and fire but God was not in them. He came in the still, small voice. We have to stop talking and doing things to hear that voice! Psalm 37:7 tells us to, *"Be still before the Lord and wait patiently for Him:"* Did you know that the words silent and listen have the same letters in them? We don't do the "be still and wait patiently" thing very well!

But Oh! the reward when we do be still and wait patiently! Isaiah 40:31 lifts us up with *"but those who hope in the Lord will renew their strength. They will soar on wings like eagles; they will run and not grow weary, they will walk and not be faint."* Can you feel your spirit rise just reading those words? Let your spirit soar!

REFLECTIONS

"

"

7

REFLECTIONS

"

„

CAREGIVERS

So much of the focus is on the ill person that we forget about the caregivers. The caregivers may be spouse, child, sibling or parent. The task of caregiving is thrust upon them whether they feel qualified, are capable of the job or are emotionally ready to take on the job. When a child wants their mommy or daddy they are not concerned with the thought of whether the parent is emotionally ready or physically ready, they just want their parent.

Mark 2:1–5 tells us the story of the paralytic man whose friends were so determined to get him to Jesus that they made an opening in the roof and lowered him down to Jesus. That took some physical work to get the man on the roof, cut a hole in the roof and then lower the man down to Jesus.

The role of the caregiver varies. Sometimes it is just the being there with them, other times it is the hands on physical care and other times it is emotional care. The caregiver goes through the stages of denial and shock, anger, bargaining, depression and acceptance as well as the ill person. The stages may occur in sequence or they may recur, as the person moves forward and backward through the stages. The caregiver and patient will move through these emotions at different times. The caregiver is grieving the loss of the person the ill person used to be, the husband who took care of everything for her, the parent who was always the caregiver but now the roles are reversed.

The caregiver is also involved in the decision making with the ill person. Again it doesn't matter if you are qualified or ready for this, you are who the ill person wants to be there and assist in these decisions. The extended family and friends should be very supportive and assuring for the caregiver.

Psalm 46 is a triumphant confession of fearless trust in God. It seems like our world is falling apart with this illness but *"The Lord Almighty is with us; the God of Jacob is our fortress."* (verse 11)

REFLECTIONS

"

"

REFLECTIONS

"

"

HEAVENLY MINDED

" Since, then, you have been raised with Christ, set your hearts on things above, where Christ is seated at the right hand of God. Set your minds on things above, not on earthly things. "

—Colossians 3:1–2

Moving into a care facility and leaving behind our home is a hard move to make. We have spent years in accumulating the things we treasure and hold dear. We have our familiar routine in our home. Now we have to establish a new routine in the new environment. We take along the basics of life as well as the aging body that needs more physical care. Most times that body requires help and care from other people because we are no longer able to do it ourselves. This may be a short time for rehabilitation or long term.

If it is a long term situation, we cling to the hope that at some point we can return to our home and have our independence again. It is hard to let go of that hope. Finding ways to feel useful in the situation you are in is a challenge. My girl friend's father is in a care center and he peels potatoes for two cookies an hour. It gives him something to look forward to and he feels useful.

In this verse in Colossians, the apostle Paul is encouraging us to set our sights *"on things above, not on earthly things."* This world and all its things is a place that we are just passing through. We cling to this world and its things because that is what is familiar and comfortable to us. We read about heaven and have the head knowledge of it but we have not experienced it yet. *"No eye has seen, no ear has heard, no mind has conceived what God has prepared for those who love Him - but God has revealed it to us by His Spirit."* (I Corinthians 2:9b–10a) We should have two feet on earth but breathe heaven's air.

God has chosen to keep you here on earth for a time yet. He has work for you to do as well as through you. It may be how you can be a witness to the caregivers and visitors by your attitude in your circumstance. *"Therefore we do not lose heart. Though outwardly we are wasting away, yet inwardly we are being renewed day by day."* (II Corinthians 4:16)

REFLECTIONS

"

"

REFLECTIONS

"

"

NO MORE TEARS

❝ He will wipe every tear from their eyes. There will be no more death or mourning or crying or pain, for the old order of things has passed away.❞ —Revelation 21:4

With all the pain and heartache we experience in the world, it is hard to imagine not having that be a part of our lives. This verse promises us that *"the old order of things has passed away"*. So no more death or mourning or crying or pain. We weep because of the time of separation from our loved ones but we have peace when we know they have given their life to the Lord and we will joyfully see them in heaven. Our sorrow is for ourselves because we miss that person from our daily lives. They are perfectly healed, in God's presence and praising Him.

Crying has a cleansing effect on us. We cry when we are in pain, we cry when we are sad, we cry when we are happy. In His earthly ministry, Jesus did His share of crying. John 11:35 simply states, *"Jesus wept"*. He was quietly grieving the loss of Lazarus, a dear friend as well as grieving for the sisters, Mary and Martha, loss.

What comfort for those who are struggling with health issues, recently lost loved ones to death or those who are looking to step into the presence of the Lord soon. Revelation 7:17 tells us that *"God will wipe away every tear from their eyes."* Those last earthly tears will be gently wiped away by our loving heavenly Father. Because there will be no tears in heaven!

Psalm 30:5 tells us, *"weeping may remain for a night, but rejoicing comes in the morning."* We weep for the sadness, hurting and separation from loved ones that we experience here on earth but joy comes in the morning when we see Jesus in heaven and He wipes the tears from our eyes.

REFLECTIONS

"

"

REFLECTIONS

"

"

PET POWER

Missy was my calico cat and we enjoyed 12 years together. I was single and she was my baby. She had five beautiful kittens and we found good homes for them. She slept with me, ate with me, traveled with me when possible and was my good buddy. When I got married she moved with me to Michigan and had to adjust to a man who teased her and wouldn't let her sleep with me. At the age of 12 her kidney's shut down and she went to her final resting place.

I was heart broken to lose my little buddy and my last tie to my life before I was married. I grieved and sought comfort. One night I had a dream that Missy was sitting on my paternal grandmother's lap in heaven. Now Grandma didn't tolerate animals in the house and I never saw her hold one. But what comfort for me that Missy and Grandma were together in heaven!

The Bible has many references to animals. God chose to save the animals in the ark with Noah's family in Genesis 7. There is no mention that any plants were saved, just animals and Noah's family. God created animals on the sixth day of creation (Genesis 1:24–25) just before He created man. *"And God saw that is was good."*

What wonderful companions animals make and I am so thankful that God gave us that relationship. Animals are known to help people with emotional and physical ailments. The calming effect they have on humans can make blood pressure drop, anxiety disappear and bring smiles to faces that have forgotten how to smile. Dogs and cats are used very effectively as therapy visitors in hospitals and care centers.

Elderly people can slip into depression when they feel no one "needs" them anymore. The responsibility and companionship of a pet can give the person new meaning to life. Taking a dog for a walk is good therapy for both human and animal. The comfort of a cat's purr lets the person know there is life and unconditional love there for them.

So share a corner of your prayer shawl with your favorite animal and thank God that He gave us those faithful companions that give us unconditional love.

REFLECTIONS

"

"

REFLECTIONS

"

"

PRAYING FOR ME

" Therefore confess your sins to each other and pray for each other so that you may be healed. The prayer of a righteous man is powerful and effective. " —James 5:16

Brian had been raised in the church, but after high school, marriage and divorce he had fallen away from the church. He had smoked for years and discovered he had a sore in his mouth that was cancerous. As a father, Brian had a son to take care of, and cancer was not good news.

Brian had surgery on his mouth in Ann Arbor, Michigan. A shawl was given to Brian through his sister's church, Central Wesleyan. He took the shawl with him to the hospital. When he returned home he put the shawl on the back of his couch. "When I look at the shawl I think of all the people who are praying for me," he said.

The prayer shawl is a tangible thing to show God's love. While the person is making the shawl, they are praying for the person who will receive the shawl. This can be great encouragement to someone who is too physically weak or discouraged to be able to pray for themselves. It also represents the caring and nourishing that we, as Christians, can do for each other as well as reaching out to those who do not know Jesus.

What comfort to know that you are not alone in your situation. Christians are interceding on your behalf before the throne of God. Your name is being brought to the throne by many different people and asking for different things for you—to heal you, emotionally uphold you, comfort you and for God's peace.

REFLECTIONS

"

"

27

REFLECTIONS

"

"

HE KNOWS MY NAME

When a prayer shawl is made, the name of the receiver is not always known. God knows! He knows your situation, who you are, He knows your name!

In this day and age we are so easily known by numbers. We are known by our social security number, car license number, driver's license number or birth date. Some families refer to their children by what number they are in birth order. But God knows me by name! John 10:27 tells us *"My sheep listen to my voice; I know them, and they follow me."* The shepherd walks ahead and the sheep follow.

What comfort and reassurance to be following the Shepherd. He leads us to the water, where there is grass and a safe place to sleep. Read Psalm 23 again and see how the Lord provides for us. On days when we are overwhelmed with decisions, we can rest in the Shepherd's care and know He will do what is best for us. Even if you had been the only one, Jesus still would have come . . . for you.

When first moving to a new area of the country, it takes awhile to establish friendships and relationships. We long for the familiarity of dialing a phone number and the person knowing our voice without having to introduce ourselves. Or meeting someone familiar at the store that we can chat with. We long to be known by our name and when that name is said with love we feel so cared for. A constant in a Christian's life is that the Shepherd knows my name!

The name our parents chose for us was in God's plan long before our birth. But not until we make the decision to make Jesus the Lord of our life, will we recognize the voice of the Shepherd. Then will our name be written in the Lamb's book of life. Revelation 21:27 tells us, *"but only those whose names are written in the Lamb's book of life"* are allowed to enter heaven.

Make Jesus the Lord of your life and then rest content, knowing that He knows your name and hears when you call on Him.

"The Lord is my shepherd, I shall not
be in want.
He makes me lie down in green pastures,
He leads me beside quiet waters,
He restores my soul.
He guides me in paths of righteousness
for His name's sake.
Even though I walk
through the valley of the shadow of death,
I will fear no evil,
for You are with me,
Your rod and Your staff, they comfort me.
You prepare a table before me
in the presence of my enemies.
You anoint my head with oil,
my cup overflows.
Surely goodness and love will follow me
all the days of my life,
and I will dwell in the house of the
Lord forever."

—Psalm 23

REFLECTIONS

"

„

I CAN DO ALL THINGS

" I can do everything through Him who gives me strength. " —Philippians 4:13

Have you found yourself in a difficult situation and feel that it is overwhelming? It can be a situation at work, health issues, difficult decisions about other people in your life or business decisions.

The story of Joseph in Genesis 37–41 brings to mind many of those situations. It hardly seems possible for all those unfortunate things to happen to one person. He was first a victim of his brothers when they sold him, then of Potiphar and his wife and then Pharaoh. He was in and out of prison for things he didn't do. Yet he maintained his high character and remained faithful to the Lord. He certainly could have used this verse as encouragement.

When dealing with a difficult circumstance we can repeat this verse in our mind and accent a different word every time. Then focus on the word we accent.

I – *"I praise You because I am fearfully and wonderfully made."* Psalm 139:14. You created just one person like me—ME. I am unique and special in God's eyes.

Can – I need to be willing to do His work, a "can do" attitude. God made me physically able to do what He has planned for me.

Do – God gave me the ability and talent to do things.

Everything – God gave me the ability to do every thing He asks of me not just some things.

Through – I am His instrument, He can work through me.

Him – The Almighty God is using me.

Who – God is the who

Gives – *"I will strengthen you and help you."* Isaiah 41:10. I am not in this alone.

Me – He knows me personally, my strengths and my weaknesses.

Strength – God's strength is in me and His strength is limitless.

Isaiah 41:10 tells us, *"So do not fear, for I am with you; do not be dismayed, for I am your God. I will strengthen you and help you; I will uphold you with my righteous right hand."* There are many verses in the Bible that refer to God's strength. Rest in the assurance from Psalm 29:11 *"The Lord gives strength to His people; the Lord blesses His people with peace."* Rest in that peace and feel God's strength in you.

REFLECTIONS

"

"

MEAT AND POTATOES

❝ In reply Jesus declared, "I tell you the truth, no one can see the kingdom of God unless he is born again.**❞**   —John 3:3

My husband is a meat and potatoes man. He grew up in a family of eight children and potatoes were an economical way to fill those growing children's tummies. My husband and I went on a low carbohydrate diet a few years ago and after a few days he had potato withdrawal and leg cramps from the decrease of potassium intake. So his portion of potatoes increased again.

What are the meat and potatoes of your spiritual life? Having a prayer shawl to wrap around you is comforting and reassuring, but have you made Jesus the Lord of your life? Are you enjoying a personal relationship with Him? That is the real meat and potatoes of life.

Salvation by faith is available to everyone who accepts Jesus as personal Savior and Lord. By faith we receive the forgiveness of our sins and the gift of eternal life; by faith we become righteous before God. And this salvation involves not merely receiving something from God; it also involves living for God in the power of the Holy Spirit.

God gave us the plan of salvation. First we have to acknowledge that we have sinned. *"All have sinned and fall short of the glory of God."* (Romans 3:23) It is easy to say, *"I am a good person"* but we are still sinners. Then Romans 6:23 tells us, *"The wages of sin is death, but the gift of God is eternal life in Christ Jesus our Lord."* Jesus was sent to earth to die for our sins as Romans 4:25 says, *"(Jesus) was delivered over to death for our sins and was raised to life for our justification."* Then comes the peace from Romans 5:1 *"Since we have been justified through faith, we have peace with God through our Lord Jesus Christ."* We are then reassured, *"Therefore, there is now no condemnation for those who are in Christ Jesus."* (Romans 8:1)

After we have acknowledged our sin and God freely gives us salvation, we will want to serve our risen Lord, *"Therefore, I urge you, brothers, in view of God's mercy, to offer your bodies as living sacrifices, holy and pleasing to God—this is your spiritual act of worship. Do not conform any longer to the pattern of this world, but be transformed by the renewing of your mind, Then you will be able to test and approve what God's will is—His good, pleasing and perfect will."* (Romans 12:1–2)

Now we can enjoy the fellowship with our Lord for He has promised in Hebrews 12:5b, *"Never will I leave you; never will I forsake you."* Feed daily on His Word, the heavenly meat and potatoes. "Life without God is like an unsharpened pencil—it has no point." Billy Graham

REFLECTIONS

"

"

REFLECTIONS

"

„

BREATHLESS BABIES

> We never touched your tiny face,
>   But in our hearts it's you we embrace.
>
>   We never heard your newborn cry,
>   Instead we're asking God "why?"
>
>   We never saw your gentle smile,
>   But you'll always be our little child.
>
>   Even though we're worlds apart,
>   We hold you close within our hearts.
>
>   We place you now in God's strong arms,
>   Safe from worries, safe from harms.
>
>   And when in heaven again we meet,
>   Then, my child, we'll be complete.

There are many babies that never drew an earthly breath. There are those that are lost early in the pregnancy by miscarriage and those that are stillborn. Each is a precious soul that slipped away to heaven.

The miscarriages that happen early in the pregnancy that most people are not aware of are sometimes not even acknowledged. The parents were aware and do their grieving privately. One way to acknowledge the child is to create a memorial of your own for the child. Use the above verse, include names that have been chosen for the child, Bible verses that were meaningful and create a card or folder. It is the parents choice whether to display it or keep it private. They can talk about it when they are ready. It is amazing once you talk to people about a miscarriage, how many people have experienced it in their lives.

The parents had a longer pregnancy to bond with a stillborn child. They felt the baby's movement and had more time to plan for the coming child. Their grief may be more acknowledged by people because more people were aware of the pregnancy. Losing a child that was still born is never easy in whatever circumstance. The "if only" and "what if" questions stay with parents for a life time. Acknowledge the birth date and allow grief to be expressed. Always be aware that God is in control of every situation and you have a child in Heaven with Jesus.

Isaiah 65 is telling us about the new heaven and new earth and verse 20 tells us, *"Never again will there be in it (heaven) an infant who lives but a few days."* When we get to heaven we will be able to get acquainted with those little ones that we did not get to spend time with here on earth.

REFLECTIONS

"

"

REFLECTIONS

"

_____

_____

_____

_____

_____

_____

_____

_____

_____

_____

_____

_____

_____

_____

_____

_____

_____

_____

_____

_____

_____

_____

_____

_____

_____

_____

_____

_____

_____

"

INFERTILITY

> " . . . and the Lord had closed her womb. "
> —I Samuel 1:5

There are many people who are experiencing infertility but it is a painful subject to talk about. Every month they experience the pain of disappointment when their cycle shows itself. We have the benefit of medical intervention that can assist in conceiving a child but sometimes there are physical reasons why a couple cannot conceive that cannot be overcome.

The Bible gives several instances of women who were barren. Sarah and Abraham waited many years to have Isaac. They took matters into their own hands in their attempt to rectify the situation. Jacob and Rebekah were not able to conceive for a time. Genesis 30 talks about Rebekah struggle with infertility and in verse 22 it states, *"Then God remembered Rachel, He opened her womb. She became pregnant and gave birth to a son."* Hannah and Elkanah were unable to have children until later. In each of these relationships, there were second wives who were able to have children, adding to the despair of the barren wife. Luke 1 gives us a New Testament story of Elizabeth's infertility before having John the Baptist. Verse 7 says, *"But they had no children, because Elizabeth was barren; and they were both well along in years."*

It is easy for the couple to begin to wonder what is the matter with them physically and sometimes that is what can be corrected by the medical world. The husband feels the pain of being unable to reproduce and to see the pain his wife is feeling and they are both longing to have a child. Many of the infertility medications make a woman's hormones unbalanced and they become more emotional about life. That can cause strain on the marriage relationship as well as other relationships.

We need to support these couples emotionally as well as lift them up in prayer. They don't need our questions and we don't need to know the details of the situation. We just need to be emotionally and prayerfully supportive. We can support them by listening if they want to talk but that has to be their choice. So many conversations are centered around how many children a person has and what their children and grandchildren are doing. Mother's Day and Father's Day are painful days for many people.

Let us pray for couples who long to be parents. May they be aware that in His time, He makes all things beautiful. May they have peace in what our Lord has for them.

REFLECTIONS

"

"

47

REFLECTIONS

"

"

SINGLE

"'Tis better to have loved and lost than to be married and be bossed." There are many different comments about being single. "Unclaimed jewels" "Late bloomers" There are many people who have never married, either by their choice or circumstance. They have just not met a person who they would care to spend the rest of their life with. Some choose careers instead of marriage or have other interests that do not include marriage.

We are not to judge these people for their choices. A single person is a whole, complete person. The painfulness of being single comes from the pressure from relatives and friends who make them feel less than complete because they are single. God created them just as they are and we need to validate them just as they are.

People mean to be helpful by arranging blind dates, giving advice of how the single person should change their hair, make up, way of dressing to be more attractive to the opposite sex. The single person is made to feel less than acceptable as they are and feel they should change just to get a partner. But God made you just as you are! You are made in His image and He has a delightful plan for your life! Bloom where you are planted!

Jesus was a single person for the entire 33 years He lived on earth. As far as we know, the apostle Paul was a single person. In I Corinthians 7:34, Paul talks about how a single woman *"is concerned about the Lord's affairs: Her aim is to be devoted to the Lord in both body and spirit."* In verse 32 Paul talks about *"an unmarried man is concerned about the Lord's affairs—how he can please the Lord."* Being single does give a person more freedom for different things.

When dating someone and considering marriage, be aware of Paul's words in II Corinthians 6:14 *"Do not be yoked together with unbelievers."* Frequently people think they can be an evangelist in dating an unbeliever. Choose Christians to date! *"What does a believer have in common with an unbeliever?"* verse 15 asks us. It is not likely that marriage will convert them to Christianity. Consider how you would like your home environment to be as well as who you want to be the father or mother of your children.

This devotional is not written to make single people think they are hurting people but to those who put undue pressure on single people to fit in by marrying. A very well adjusted single person can make a miserably married person very uncomfortable. Romans 12:6 tells us, *"We have different gifts, according to the grace given us."* If God gave you the gift of singleness for how ever long, let your light shine that God may be glorified through you!

REFLECTIONS

"

"

REFLECTIONS

"

"

LOSS THROUGH DEATH

God makes the choice when death claims a beloved spouse or child. There is never an easy time of life to lose a spouse to death. Young spouses with young children struggle to understand why God took a spouse and parent when the children are at an age when they so need that parent. Children and teenagers need their parents and it is hard to understand God's plan in taking a parent. We plan to grow old with that beloved spouse but God took them before we arrived to that stage of life. We question God's wisdom in taking these loved ones "before their time". The surviving spouse struggles to find a new normal in their world. We have to rest in the comfort and knowledge that God is in control and He knows best. Job 1:21 states, *"Naked I came from my mother's womb and naked I will depart. The Lord gave and the Lord has taken away; may the name of the Lord be praised."* Job's faith leads him to see the sovereign God's hand at work, and that gives him peace in the face of calamity. Lamentations 3:32–33 tells us, *"Though He brings grief, He will show compassion, so great is His unfailing love. For He does not willingly bring affliction or grief to the children of men."* The same God who judges also restores. God's faithfulness and unfailing love are used together to sum up God's covenant mercies toward His people.

Losing children to death at any age is not easy. Our thought is parents die first but that isn't always what God has in His plan for us. Watching a child suffer with illness over a period of time takes it's toll on the parents as well as the siblings of the child. David watched his infant son that he had with Bathsheba suffer and die in II Samuel 12:15–23. He was dealing with his sin of adultery as well as grieving the death of his child. Then in II Samuel 18, David receives the news that his adult son Absalom has been killed in battle. David grieved for his son in spite of all the grief that Absalom had been to his father in his life time.

The story of Ruth and Naomi tells us how difficult life was for widows. They were at the mercy of any male relative. Financially they were totally dependent until Boaz chose to marry Ruth and then he was responsible for Naomi as well.

Our Lord sent His Son to earth, knowing what a cruel death He would endure. Our heavenly Father grieved that loss as well as grieved for the people who were doing this to Him.

The great comfort that Christians can rest in is knowing their loved one is now at home with the Lord. They will not return to us but we will go to join them in our heavenly home.

REFLECTIONS

"

"

REFLECTIONS

"

"

SINGLE AGAIN

There are many people who find themselves single again through the loss of their partner through divorce. They find themselves in these circumstances not always by their choice.

Divorce is a painful thing especially to the spouse who had married for life and did not choose to divorce. It is painful for the partner who has to choose divorce due to abuse, abandonment, or infidelity. They suffer with their own pain, grief and betrayal as well as the pain and grief their children are struggling to understand why their parents are no longer living together. The family deals with grief for the loss of relationships as they had hoped they would be. Philippians 3:13–14 tells us, *"Forgetting what is behind and straining toward what is ahead, I press on toward the goal to win the prize for which God has called me heavenward in Christ Jesus."* We must forgive ourselves as God has forgiven us and set our sights on Him.

God does advise us to remain sexually pure when we are not married. Hebrews 13:4 says, *"Marriage should be honored by all and the marriage bed kept pure, for God will judge the adulterer and all the sexually immoral."* When we are not married we are to abstain from sex. If we marry again, then we can present ourselves to that new partner pure from having sex with someone we were not married to. God reserves sex for marriage. I Corinthians 6:19–20 tells us, *"Do you not know that your body is a temple of the Holy Spirit, who is in you, whom you have received from God? You are not your own; you were bought at a price. Therefore honor God with your body."*

Our society and especially the church, are hard on people who divorce. We tend to judge harshly when we should be loving them into the fold. Usually they are struggling with financial problems and trying to find themselves as a single person. Friendships that were made as couples are now strained and they find themselves looking for new friendships.

The visitation schedule for children between the parents is a stressor for the parents, children and any new spouses involved. The parents are struggling to not put the children in the middle of the strife. Rules, values and behavior is different in the different parent's homes and dealing with step siblings adds stress to both children and adults.

We can see how God says in Malichi 2:16, *"I hate divorce"* because of all the heartache it causes. But there are people who cannot stay in a relationship due to infidelity or abuse that makes it a physically unsafe place for them to be for themselves and their children.

Psalm 23:4 tells us, *"Even though I walk THROUGH the valley…"* It doesn't say God walks us into the valley but through the valley. God is with you as you walk through this difficult time in your life. The verse goes on to say, "Your rod and Your staff they comfort me." The rod and staff symbolize the instrument of authority that is used in counting, guiding, rescuing and protecting. God is there with you, comforting and guiding you as you search out your future.

REFLECTIONS

"

"

CHRONIC PAIN

Chronic pain is defined as " a disease or disorder developing slowly and persisting for a long period, often for the remainder of a person's lifetime" in Mosby's Medical Dictionary. An individual dealing with chronic pain may withdraw from family, friends and environment, concentrating solely on their pain. Pain makes us irritable and that puts stress on relationships. There is a feeling of hopelessness and wanting life to end.

There are unending appointments for doctors, therapists and various medications and treatments in an attempt to decrease or control the pain. After spending a restless night dealing with pain, morning comes and we are forced to face the day with the continuing pain. Friends and family grow weary of hearing complaints of pain. They try to be supportive but it is one of those situations that until you have walked in that person's shoes, you really don't understand. It is hard to focus on anything, sometimes the eye sight is affected and sometimes the brain is unable to focus on anything except the pain. We wish for release from our earthly suffering and be perfectly healed in Heaven.

In II Corinthians 12:7, Paul talks about *"there was given me a thorn in my flesh"*. We are not sure of the nature of this affliction but it may be a chronic pain that he endured. Later in verses 8 and 9 he says, *"Three times I pleaded with the Lord to take it away from me. But He said to me, My Grace is sufficient for you, for my power is made perfect in weakness."* Our human weakness provides the ideal opportunity for the display of Divine power.

When we are suffering with pain that brings us to our knees, it is hard to focus on anything but our pain. Paul urges us to boast about our weakness and for Christ's sake to delight in it. That is pretty hard to do when we are miserable with pain! We would rather curl up with our prayer shawl and shut the world out.

Recently I experienced several years of intense chronic pain. I did not realize how much of my personality had changed during the time of experiencing the pain. I was trying to function as best I could with the pain by going to work, doing my job and trying to be pleasant. I was written up for a negative attitude at work in spite of my efforts. I had surgery and that greatly relieved the pain. My boss commented about my improved attitude but no explaining on my part could convey to him how miserable I had been with the pain. I am trying to focus on being thankful that there was something that could be done to relieve my pain and have a cheerful attitude.

Our God gives us comfort and reassurance in Isaiah 40 and then in verse 31 He tells us, *"but those who hope in the Lord will renew their strength. They will soar on wings like eagles; they will run and not grow weary, they will walk and not be faint."* Our weakness will give way to God's strength. The eagle is known for its vigor and speed. Amidst our pain it is hard to fathom to run let alone not get weary and to walk and not faint when most days walking is a struggle. Verse 28 b of Isaiah 40 tells that *"He (God) will not grow tired or weary, and His understanding no one can fathom."* He knows and understands our pain and He is always there with us.

REFLECTIONS

"

"

DEPRESSION

"As they pass through the Valley of Baca, they make it a place of springs; the autumn rains also cover it with pools." —Psalm 84:6

Depression is something most of us have dealt with from time to time in our life. For some it is short term that once the situation that created the depression has passed, life can move to a happier note. For others it is a life time of dealing with sadness and fighting the blackness that wants to envelop you. Mosby's Medical dictionary talks about depression being "an abnormal emotional state characterized by exaggerated feelings of sadness, melancholy, dejection, worthlessness, emptiness and hopelessness that are inappropriate and out of proportion to reality." Psalm 84:6 refers to depression as the "Valley of Baca". The Valley of Baca is not a place on the map, it is a figurative place. It is a dry, arid stretch that pilgrims have to traverse to get to the places of refreshment that God provides on our journey. God can help us make our Valley of Baca a place of refreshment, encouragement and drawing closer to Him.

Post postpartum depression is something that new mothers sometimes deal with after having a baby. The hormones in their bodies are adjusting to a non-pregnant state. The new mother feels guilty for feeling blue and spends a lot of time crying. She has a healthy new baby and life should be wonderful. Loving affirmation from her husband and family just doesn't seem to be enough.

People that live in the northern United States can experience seasonal affective disorder (SAD) especially during winter months. The overcast, cold, short days of sunlight and long nights of darkness can make people depressed. The weather limits outside activity and keeps people inside most of the winter months.

Depressed people will isolate from life. We build emotional walls around ourselves to prevent further infliction of pain from those around us. Finally we feel numb, we have no emotions, no feelings because that would cause more pain. Depression can be seen as the black pit of despair that traps us emotionally. Job experienced depression and in chapter 3:11–14 he questions why he was even born. Later in chapter 3:21 he talks about longing for death.

In I Kings 19:3–20:18 we are given the story when Elijah became discouraged and ran away from what God had planned for him to do. God allowed him to sleep and then fed him, allowed him to sleep some more and then fed him again. Then God had a serious talk with Elijah as to why he was feeling this way. We need to see to those basic needs for ourselves and others. We become run down from lack of sleep, too busy and expecting too much from ourselves.

Then Satan moves in and plants doubts in our minds about what has happened, who said what, why it was done and on and on! We need to seek out a person or a counselor that we can trust to talk to. Many of us process our emotions when we verbalize them. We need to be available to others to be that confidential person they can talk to.

Many of David's Psalms talk about how the world is out to get David and then the last verses are praise to God. Psalm 7 talks about David's enemies (Saul) trying to kill him. Verse 17 says, *"I will give thanks to the Lord because of His righteousness and will sing praise to the name of the Lord."* Psalm 43:2 questions, *"Why must I go about mourning, oppressed by the enemy?"* and verse 5 answers with, *"Why are you downcast, O my soul? Why so disturbed within me? Put your hope in God, for I will yet praise Him, my Savior and my God."* We need to drink deep from His Word to make our Valley of Baca a place of refreshment, encouragement and drawing closer to Him as we continue our journey through life.

REFLECTIONS

"

"

SONGS IN THE NIGHT

Many of us have experienced insomnia, not being able to sleep at night. Sometimes we are unable to fall asleep and sometimes we wake after a few hours of sleep. We wake for many different reasons and sometimes it seems no reason at all. Pain, fear, full bladder, children crying, spouse snoring or restlessness can all be part of the reason we are awake. Our first thought is, "why am I awake?"

In the dark hours of the night, all the troubles of the day seem to get largely out of perspective. The pain seems more intense, loneliness seems engulfing and prayers seem to barely get to the ceiling. There seems to be more sounds that we are aware of and if there is a storm raging outside as well as inside, it seems overwhelming.

Frequently when we are awakened, someone is on our mind. We must not minimize those thoughts, God woke you and put them on your mind for a purpose. For what ever reason, God may be asking you to pray for them. We don't know what is going on in their life at that moment but God sure does! All the other thoughts have not made you peaceful to fall asleep but praying seems to be very calming and shortly we are asleep again.

God frequently gives us thoughts of a song or a verse in scripture. What a blessing those thoughts are! Sadly those aren't our first thoughts when we waken! Isaiah 26:9 tells us, *"My soul yearns for you in the night."* The book of Psalms is full of verses and promises about insomnia so this is not a new issue in the life of God's people. Psalm 63:6 says, *"On my bed I remember You; I think of You through the watches of the night."*

Many of these devotionals have been written in the night. God woke me up with a thought or a verse and I felt I needed to get them written down immediately as by morning they would be gone. While I was researching another devotion I came on the verse from Psalm 119:148, *"My eyes stay open through the watches of the night, that I may meditate on Your promises."* When I think of all the rich blessings God has given me while I am searching His Word during the night, I am so thankful that I was obedient to Him to get up and write things down.

The best promise from God is found in Psalm 121:3–4, *"He will not let your foot slip—He who watches over you will not slumber; indeed, He who watches over Israel will neither slumber nor sleep."* The Lord of all creation is the One in whom the faithful may put unfaltering trust is alert and attentive at all times. Then we can do as Psalm 4:8 says, *"I will lie down and sleep in peace, for you alone, O Lord, make me dwell in safety."* Rest comfortably and peacefully in His almighty arms. The arms of our Lord that hold the whole universe are holding you tonight. He will never let you go.

REFLECTIONS

"

"

REFLECTIONS

"

"

ONE STEP CLOSER TO HEAVEN

" Therefore we do not lose heart. Though outwardly we are wasting away, yet inwardly we are being renewed day by day. For our light and momentary troubles are achieving for us an eternal glory that far outweighs them all. So we fix our eyes not on what is seen, but on what is unseen. For what is seen is temporary, but what is unseen is eternal. " —II Corinthians 4:16–18

When my uncle was diagnosed with ALS (Lou Gehrig's disease) he claimed these verses. While he was breathing his last breaths, my aunt read these verses to him.

Receiving a diagnosis of cancer or a terminal illness is never easy. The first human reaction is numbness and disbelief as the facts begin to sink in and we learn more about the diagnosis. We are aware that these earthly bodies are not forever and we do not know the path that God has chosen for us to follow regarding our death. These "light and momentary troubles" seem pretty overwhelming from our earthly perspective.

The family as well as the person with the diagnosis begin a journey that includes denial and shock, anger, bargaining, depression and acceptance. Each individual moves forward and backward through these stages. The Christian has the comfort from Hebrews 13:5–6, *"God has said, Never will I leave you; never will I forsake you. So we say with confidence, The Lord is my helper; I will not be afraid. What can man do to me?"* The process of dying is scary to our earthly minds. We fear what illness we will have to go through before we are released from this suffering and be present with the Lord. We have our eyes fixed on what we see and know.

James 5:14–16 talks about praying to be healed. God certainly can heal whether it be through traditional medicine or divine intervention. Sometimes He heals us perfectly in heaven. The disciples were given the power to heal and cast out demons in Mark 6:13 and God worked very mightily through them. Deuteronomy 32:4 reassures us with, *"He is the Rock, His works are perfect, and all His ways are just. A faithful God who does no wrong, upright and just is He."*

There are times when our prayers seem not to go beyond the ceiling. We are emotionally and physically exhausted. Physical illness makes it hard to think clearly and process thoughts. God is there with you! Romans 8:26–27 reassures us, *"In the same way, the Spirit helps us in our weakness. We do not know what we ought to pray for, but the Spirit Himself intercedes for us with groans that words cannot express. And He who searches our hearts knows the mind of the Spirit, because the Spirit intercedes for the saints in accordance with God's will."* The prayer shawl that was made for you is a tangible thing that reminds you of the prayers that are being said on your behalf. Surround yourself with praying friends and family.

Experiencing a terminal illness gives us time to put our life in order. It is a gradual letting go of earthly people and things that we hold so dear. Gradually our focus turns more to eternal things and heaven. Job 19:25–27 tells us, *"I know that my Redeemer lives and that in the end He will stand upon the earth. And after my skin has been destroyed, yet in my flesh I will see God; I myself will see Him with my own eyes—I, and not another. How my heart yearns within me!"* These clenched fists that grasp so tightly to this earth, gradually open up to receive the reward of heaven.

REFLECTIONS

"

"

NO WORRIES, MATE!

The Australian's have this wonderful phrase, "No Worries, Mate!" That is their way of saying to not worry about something, don't concern yourself, it will be taken care of! We tend to take life so seriously and worry about things that might happen, did happen or never will happen. Recently I found a phrase that states, "Don't let your worries get the best of you; Remember Moses started out as a basket case." Those are humble beginnings for a person who became God's choice to lead His people out of Egypt.

There is a little song that goes, "Why worry when you can pray? Trust Jesus. He'll be your stay. Don't be a doubting Thomas, rest fully on His promise. Why worry, worry, worry, when you can pray." Matthew 6:19–34 talks about worrying and verse 27 especially says *"Who of you by worrying can add a single hour to his life."* That just shows us how futile worry is. It doesn't change a thing and we lose a lot of sleep, peace and productive time in life by worrying. God is in control and we need to leave it with Him and rest in Him.

In Psalm 139:19 David is wanting to tell God what to do. *"If only you would slay the wicked, O God!"* He is impatient with God's patience toward the wicked. Their end will come in God's time. Isaiah 11 talks about God's justice and how He won't just judge by what He sees or hears, He will judge with righteousness. So why are we worrying about things that God has totally under control and it is not ours to judge anyway? Worry is a lack of trust in our Heavenly Father.

There is a saying, "Worry is interest on a loan not yet borrowed." We are running way ahead of God and the situation with our worrying. Matthew 6:34 instructs us, *"Therefore do not worry about tomorrow, for tomorrow will worry about itself. Each day has enough trouble of its own."*

What we worry about today may not even be the issue tomorrow.

It is easy to worry about our world situation, politics and concern for the next generation and how their world will be. God is in control of all of that. He is allowing this all to happen and we are not to know what the end of it will be. Psalm 37 tells us, *"do not fret"* over these things, God is in control! Read Psalm 37 in it's entirety and be reassured of God's care.

We spend a lot of time worrying about our health, our children's health, money, what is happening at work and many more things. "Why worry when you can pray?" We as Christian's have that wonderful option that we bring our cares to Jesus and LEAVE THEM THERE!

REFLECTIONS

"

"

79

REFLECTIONS

"

,,

AGED TO PERFECTION

Growing old isn't for sissies! One elderly gentleman was heard to say, "getting old is downright inconvenient". The golden years don't feel so golden with all the aches and pains that come with it.

Solomon talks about aging in Ecclesiastes 12:2–5 using symbolism about parts of the body deteriorating. The grinders are teeth and how eating becomes difficult, windows are eyes that the vision grows dim, doors to the streets is referring to parts of the body such as hands and feet that no longer work as well as they used to and the almond tree's pale blossom refers to the white hair of age. The grasshopper, who is normally agile, dragging himself is referring to the stiffness of old age. The aging body requires more care and all the aches and pains are discouraging.

My 87 year old neighbor lady wanted to get a new vehicle while she was young enough to learn to use it. She is happily driving her new vehicle. Old age is a state of mind, if you don't mind it doesn't matter.

The aging process also affects the mind in different ways. We get more forgetful and it becomes more difficult to recall things. We become anxious about not being able to remember things. God is there with you in that as well.

A part of the aging process also includes not being able to care for ourselves and having to move to a care facility or have someone come into our home to help care for us. Having someone else do the things that we have done for ourselves for so many years is an adjustment. As we age, changes are harder to do and adjusting to changes is more difficult. Leaving the home that we have spent years living in is difficult. We have a lot of memories as well as things that we have to leave behind. We know it is earthly things, but that doesn't make them any less dear to us.

Job 12:12 tells us, *"Is not wisdom found among the aged? Does not long life bring understanding?"* We are too soon old and too late smart! The wisdom that experience has taught people throughout their life is a wealth of knowledge that younger people would be wise to tap into. A lot of it is the common sense kind of understanding of life.

Leviticus 19:32 says *"Rise in the presence of the aged, show respect for the elderly and revere your God. I am the Lord."* We are to show respect for the elderly. We can do that by listening to them respectfully, assisting them with a helping hand with daily activities and giving words of encouragement. If you have enjoyed a long term relationship with an elderly person, you know their likes and dislikes, sense of humor and have many happy memories with them. Help them to recall those memories and enjoy the walk down memory lane together. Those of us who are young now have to appreciate that our future may include growing old.

REFLECTIONS

"

"

HANDS TO WORK, HEARTS TO GOD

> **❝** Moreover, when God gives any man wealth and possessions, and enables him to enjoy them, to accept his lot and be happy in his work—this is a gift of God. **❞** —Ecclesiastes 5:19

Our job, career or occupation seem to define who we are. It is good to take pride in our job and what we do but it shouldn't define our whole being. It is important that whatever we do, we do our best. Colossians 3:17 tells us, *"whatever you do, whether in word or deed, do it all in the name of the Lord Jesus, giving thanks to God the Father through Him."* We are not only to do our work well, we are to be thankful that we have work to do.

Losing a job by being fired or laid off is very difficult. The loss of financial income and the emotional feelings of inadequacy chip away at our self esteem. Having no job then gives a person a lot of time to think and one becomes your own worst enemy. Job hunting is a discouraging and humbling "job" to do and we again struggle with self esteem issues when we are not called back by an employer for an interview or are told that we were not the one they chose to hire.

When we have a job that we dislike and are unhappy doing the job but it does pay a good wage and pays the bills, we feel guilty for feeling this way. It is hard to keep a positive attitude at a job that we are not enjoying. When the boss calls you into the office to have a discussion about your attitude, you know it is time for a change on your part to adjust the attitude or look for another job. Proverbs 31 gives us a job description of a woman who, by earthly standards, is perfect. She is able to do everything, it would seem, and have a positive attitude about it all.

We need jobs for the income it gives us to survive. Ecclesiastes 5:10 gives us these words of wisdom, *"Whoever loves money never has money enough; whoever loves wealth is never satisfied with his income. This too is meaningless."* How much value and self worth do we put into what possessions we have or how much money we have? Where should our value and self worth come from? Ecclesiastes 5 goes on to say, *"As goods increase, so do those who consume them. And what benefit are they to the owner except to feast his eyes on them?"* How often we see wealthy people with lots of "friends" but when the wealth goes away, so do the "friends".

This brings us around full circle to why we are working and what is our purpose here on earth. John 6:27 advises us to, *"Do not work for food that spoils, but for food that endures to eternal life, which the Son of Man will give you. On him God the Father has placed His seal of approval."* We need to step back and see the bigger picture and not be so focused on our little corner of the world. God would have us be happy in our jobs but our ultimate happiness is *"to prepare God's people for works of service, so that the body of Christ may be built up"* (Ephesians 4:12).

REFLECTIONS

"

"

CROSSING JORDAN

"When I come to the river at ending of day,
When the last winds of sorrow have blown.

There'll be Somebody waiting to show me the way
I won't have to cross Jordan alone.

I won't have to cross Jordan alone,
Jesus died for my sins to atone

In the darkness I see, He'll be waiting for me,
I won't have to cross Jordan alone."

The final breath of life is a scary thought because we are un-familiar with what will happen then. Humanly speaking, we have to do this alone. We are comfortable and familiar with where we are on this earth. We have surrounded ourselves with friends, family and our familiar environment where our earthly "treasures" are. But when it comes to the end of our life, humans cannot go with us. We all die at some time, but we still need to do this individually.

As Christians we need to look at the big picture of stepping away from this life and into the arms of Jesus. Many of us have stood at the bedside of a loved one as they near the end of life. Frequently it is said that the person dying will say Jesus' name or point to Him in the room. What comfort to know that Jesus is there waiting to take us to His heavenly home.

2 Corinthians 5:8 reassures us, *"We are confident, I say, and would prefer to be away from the body and at home with the Lord."* We will no longer be living in this earthly tent but will be at home with the Lord. And that is much preferable to our present life in this frail, human body. In these earthly bodies we struggle with physical, emotional and spiritual aches and pains but we do have the comfort of the Lord's spiritual presence with us.

I sang the above song as a solo in a music contest when I was in grade school. I did not appreciate the words until I became an adult.

In Hebrews 13:1, *"God has said, 'Never will I leave you; never will I forsake you.' So we say with confidence, 'The Lord is my helper; I will not be afraid.'"* So through the whole process of illness and dying, never will He leave us. Paul tells us, *"I eagerly expect and hope that I will in no way be ashamed, but will have sufficient courage so that now as always Christ will be exalted in my body, whether by life or by death. For to me, to live is Christ and to die is gain."* (Philippians 1:20–21). Christ dwells in these human bodies of ours and we want to honor our Lord in our living as well as in dying. Our limited eye sight sees what earthly gains we have here but think of the "gain" of heaven!! It takes crossing Jordan to get to that eternal reward.

REFLECTIONS

"

"

PARACHUTE BLANKET

Leanne's father is 95 years old and resides in a care center. He is very alert and very interested in today's events and happenings. Recently he had to be hospitalized for some health issues and Leanne called to see how he was. He told her he had received a parachute blanket from the ladies of his church. "I don't know what I need that thing for!" he commented to Leanne. Leanne was thinking it was something made out of light weight fabric that parachutes are made of. The next day her dad told her the same thing. A few days later Leanne went to visit her Dad, who lives several hours away, and he showed her his parachute blanket. It was a camouflage designed fleece blanket. Then Leanne understood that it was a prayer shawl but her Dad had understood them to say parachute blanket.

The parachute is defined in Webster's dictionary as "an apparatus of an umbrella shape with which aircraft are provided, for the purpose of enabling safe descent by crew or troops." So our prayer shawl can be used as a parachute, that is made with prayer, to assist us as we travel through a difficult time in our life. It is an uplifting feeling we get when we look at our prayer shawl and know it represents so many people praying for us.

There are so many encouraging verses in the Bible that we can claim as our parachute through difficult times. Isaiah 54:10 tells us, *"Though the mountains be shaken and the hills be removed, yet my unfailing love for you will not be shaken nor my covenant of peace be removed, says the Lord, who has compassion on you."* God can give you peace in the midst of everything that is happening. It doesn't change the diagnosis or the outcome, having God's peace just carries you through it all.

Isaiah 40:31 talks about *"but those who hope in the Lord will renew their strength. They will soar on wings like eagles."* Our earthly parachute just assists us to a safe landing back on earth. God is talking about soaring when we hope in the Lord. Webster's dictionary defines soaring as "to mount upward on wings, to rise above what is commonplace." When we soar on God's wings we will "run and not grow weary, we will walk and not be faint." Our weakness will give way to God's strength.

REFLECTIONS

"

"

REFLECTIONS

"

_____

_____

_____

_____

_____

_____

_____

_____

_____

_____

_____

_____

_____

_____

_____

_____

_____

_____

_____

_____

_____

_____

_____

_____

"

FREELY GIVEN

At the last Prayer Shawl meeting, Sherma, who loves to make baby blankets, gave me two bags of baby shawls. That evening, I received a phone call from a young man who had just been to the Family Christian Book Store and had bought the "Prayer Shawl Ponderings" devotion book. He called to ask if he could buy two prayer shawls for his newborn twin boys who were in the intensive care nursery. "I want to put them over the things that the babies are laying in," he said. I told him we did not sell the shawls, but I would get them for him.

I looked through the shawls that Sherma had given me earlier that day, and I found two blue blankets – a blue variegated one and a plain blue one. I called the father back and told him I had shawls for them. I reassured them that they did not need to pay for them, and when I told them that the person making the shawls had prayed while she made them, they were very happy to hear that. They then told me they would take a picture of the babies with the shawls and send it to me.

We have no idea if these people belong or attend a church, but they felt a need to have prayer shawls for their babies. We don't always know how our prayer shawls may be used, but we are always glad to be able to supply them, free.

In Matthew 10 Jesus is giving instructions to the disciples as they are being sent out to bring the good news of salvation to the world. In verse 8 He states, *"Freely you have received, freely give."* He is talking about material things as well as spreading the gospel and doing good deeds.

Jesus freely gave Himself to come to earth and die on the cross for our salvation. Ephesians 1:6 tells us, *"to the praise of His glorious grace, which He has freely given us in the One He loves."* He gave His life freely so we can understand, *"For the wages of sin is death, but the gift of God is eternal life in Christ Jesus our Lord."* (Romans 6:23). The gift that Jesus gave us doesn't compare to anything we can give. The tangible shawl that enfolds a person physically is minor compared to what Jesus gave. The prayers that are put into the shawl reach much further and enfold the person spiritually. *"For God so loved the world that He GAVE His one and only Son, that whoever believes in Him shall not perish but have eternal life."* (John 3:16)

REFLECTIONS

"

"

REFLECTIONS

"

"

ALZHEIMER'S

    " I tell you the truth, when you were younger you
dressed yourself and went where you wanted;
but when you are old you will stretch out your
hands, and someone else will dress you and lead
you where you do not want to go. **"** —John 21:18

As we age we can become increasingly forgetful. And as time
goes on it becomes more of a concern as we forget where we
are going while driving or walking from place to place, if we
ate dinner and people's names. Mosby's dictionary defines
Alzheimer's as "progressive mental deterioration, characterized
by confusion, memory failure, disorientation, restlessness,
speech disturbances, inability to carry out purposeful movement and hallucinosis." Many different labels are attached
such as dementia, hardening of the arteries,

When we are forgetting things that are happening we
laugh and talk about memory loss. At first we laugh and
then we laugh nervously about how much we are forgetting.
Alzheimer's is such a gradual disease that is seems to "sneak
up" on us. When the person begins to notice the memory
loss, they become very good at compensating and hiding
their loss. It is easy to isolate even when in a group of people
so they don't say something they feel is inappropriate. The

person begins to grieve the loss of their memory and the people around them are also grieving the loss of that person's memory and changes in behavior. The person feels an urgency to spend time with people they love, talk things over and get their house in order while they are still mentally alert. The alertness comes and goes so they want to make good use of the good days.

The family of the person will experience anger and confusion that the person can remember sometimes, some things and not know anything a few minutes later. Family members will react differently. Some will be in denial that their loved one has the disease and others will want to be overly helpful. Others will not want to spend time with the person so they can deny there is anything wrong or don't want to see them unable to function at their usual level. We need to make time to spend with the person, to accept the good days and celebrate them and care for them on the days they are unable to care for themselves.

My Dad was diagnosed with Alzheimer's in his 70's and is now in a care center with advanced disease. He was the kind of man who always knew which direction was east, which way we were driving and how to get there. Now he doesn't know where his room is at the care center or how to get to the dining room. He shuffles when he walks and I think of him as a younger man when he was sure footed as he did his work on the farm. I miss the person he used to be. I would like to talk things over with him that are happening in my life. But then he surprises us by coming through with some words of wisdom and his wonderful sense of humor. Not long ago he verbalized that we are not in this world to stay and how we have to let go of these earthly possessions and reach for the eternal things.

I am thankful for the legacy that my parents brought us up in a Christian home, church and school. Psalm 63:6 tells us, *"On my bed I remember you; I think of you through the watches of the night."* The long-term memory for my Dad is of his faith and trust in God. I trust that is what comes to mind for him now when his short term memory is so short. In our younger years we can be imprinting Bible verses, words to hymns and praying in our memory so they are part of our long term memory as we age. Then when something like Alzheimer's claims our short term memory we have the firm foundation in God's word for our long term memory. Many people with Alzheimer's may not be able to remember what they had for lunch but when familiar hymns are being sung or Bible verses quoted, they can repeat them word for word.

We can anticipate heaven where everything will be made clear to us. My Dad will be able to think clearly and know everyone.

REFLECTIONS

"

"

SPECIAL NEEDS PERSON

" For you created my inmost being; you knit me together in my mother's womb. I praise you because I am fearfully and wonderfully made; your works are wonderful, I know that full well. My frame was not hidden from you when I was made in the secret place. When I was woven together in the depths of the earth, your eyes saw my unformed body. " —Psalm 139:13–15

Psalm 139 is a wonderful passage about God knowing every thought, word and deed about us and from whom there is no hiding. In verse 15 it talks about our being *"made in the secret place"* which is the womb. God was there at the very beginning of our existence and He knows how we are put together. By earthly standards some of us have "flaws" but in God's eyes we are all perfect. Children that are born with a handicap or become handicapped later in life are part of God's plan. Parents feel guilt for having a child that has a handicap at birth or have something happen to them that leaves them handicapped.

In the world of special needs individuals, each person functions at their own level of mental understanding and physical abilities. If no learning or responsibilities are expected from the child, then the child doesn't learn to function at their maximum potential. How the parents respond and challenge the child is how the child will respond to others in life. It is easy for the parents to want to sympathize with a handicapped child in dealing with physical limitations and social acceptance.

Psalm 139 reassures us that God knows everything about us even before we are born, Nothing happens to us or our children that isn't part of God's plan.

My husband's daughter, Amy, was born a normal, healthy child. At age 5, on her first day of kindergarten, the bus left her off at the wrong place. Amy knew she was at the wrong place so decided to run to the babysitters house where she was supposed to have been dropped off. She attempted to cross the street and was hit by a van. She suffered closed head injuries and multiple bone fractures. She spent a month in the hospital and eight months in a rehabilitation hospital learning to eat, walk and toilet train all over again. She now functions at an 8–10 year old level of mental understanding and deals with physical limitations. She lives in a group home and enjoys the different activities there as well as interacting with her house mates and group home supervisor. She has a job and does volunteer work for a couple different agencies. It is a challenge to find work for her that she can physically and mentally handle.

Amy is content with her life. She moved into the group home when she was 18 years old. She had told her teacher, "I feel like I finally fit in." She enjoys special olympics, special ministries which is a Bible study for special needs people and doing things with the group home ladies.

Parents and guardians struggle with normal land marks in the child's life. When other children are sitting up, walking or feeding themselves, turning 16 and learning to drive, turning 21, getting married, the list goes on and on. But these children have their own land marks and we celebrate them.

Just as we are all different, special needs people have their uniqueness that makes them an individual. Some are more social and want to be with people and others would rather isolate. The challenge is to guide them to their maximum potential. Finding work and activities that they can physically and mentally handle is a challenge but the person feels so "normal" when they are productive to society.

REFLECTIONS

"

"

DISASTER

❝Naked I came from my mother's womb, and naked I will depart. The Lord gave and the Lord has taken away; may the name of the Lord be praised.❞ —Job 1:20

A few years ago we experienced a "flood" in our basement. In reality we had less than an inch of water covering the whole basement floor. We had to tear up carpet, throw out wet boxes with their contents that were soaked with dirty water. I had yarn in paper boxes on the floor and I scooped off the top yarn that wasn't wet and then had to throw the rest away. After hours of rescuing what we could and throwing out, we were exhausted. Then we watch the news where people have their basement level full of water or a tornado comes and sweeps the whole house away. They show pictures of people picking through things to find what few possessions that are intact and even broken things that are so meaningful. Frequently the comment is, "At least my family is alive."

The book of Job tells us how God allowed Satan to test Job. His oxen and camels were carried off by enemies, his sheep and servants were burned, and his children were killed. Satan also inflicted ill health on Job. Verse 22 of the first chapter says, *"In all this, Job did not sin by charging God with wrongdoing."* He questioned God about what was happening to him but he did not curse God. The book of Job goes on with the dialogue from Job's friends who were a mixture of encouragement and words that contain an element of truth and others, including his wife, encouraged him to, *"Curse God and die!"* Job spoke of his personal relationship with God while his friends spoke only about God.

So there is Job in very poor health, no emotional support from his wife or his friends. He was not aware of the interaction between God and Satan regarding his "testing". Difficult times are hard enough without the emotional support of loved ones and people who have experienced difficult times. In Job 19:25 are the wonderful words, *"I know that my Redeemer lives, and that in the end He will stand upon the earth."*

We can endure floods, tornados, sunnami, earthquakes or fires that destroy our homes and our world around us. Losing loved ones through death or other painful things that we humans inflict on each other is all part of our lives. The "acts of God" are things that happen that are totally out of human control through nature, shape our lives. These material things can be taken away from us so quickly and we grieve their loss. It is so difficult to not have an earthly home to go to! The big picture is that God is still the same today as He was before the disaster struck and He is still in control. We can question God about why things are happening to us, just as Job did, but we have to realize God is in control. Nothing happens to us without God's hand in it.

REFLECTIONS

"

"

LET YOUR LIGHT SHINE

" In the same way, let your light shine before men, that they may see your good deeds and praise your Father in heaven. " —Matthew 5:16

"Jesus bids us shine, with a clear, pure light,
Like a little candle burning in the night;

In this world of darkness, we must shine,
You in your small corner, and I in mine.

Jesus bids us shine, first of all for Him,
Well He sees and knows it, if our light is dim;

He looks down from heaven sees us shine,
You in your small corner, and I in mine.

Jesus bids us shine, then, for all around,
Many kinds of darkness in this world abound,

Sin and want and sorrow—we must shine,
You in your small corner, and I in mine.
                    —Anna B. Warner

How we react to stressful situations reflects on what kind of person we are. Our light can shine brightly when things are going well, we are healthy and all is right with the world. But what about when we become ill, are given a terminal diagnoses, changes in living arrangements and we feel like we have lost control of our lives? Are we calm and praise God for what is happening, even then?

Having worked many years in the medical world, it is interesting to observe how people react to health issues and stress. There is a peace in the room when a Christian is taking their last earthly breath and anticipates entering the presence of Jesus. When we don't feel good, it is hard to get our light to shine. A patient in any medical care facility is being observed by doctors, care givers, housekeeping and any visitors that enter the room. How we let Jesus' light shine through us in those situations speaks loudly. Angry out bursts, being rude to care givers, swearing and cursing the Lord are not good examples of letting God's light shine. We need to surround ourselves with praying believers to help us through this time.

Jesus is asking us to let our light shine, to let others see Jesus in us. He isn't asking all of us to become preachers but we can be evangelists in our little corner of the world. How we live, what we read, what we do with free time, how we react to stress are all being observed by people who are not Christians and our response speaks volumes to them.

There are many songs written about showing your light, lighting your world, let it shine and being a beacon. The hard part is bringing it to your world, going to work every day, living with the people in your home and those you spend your free time with. Matthew 5:14 tell us that we are the light of the world and verse 15 goes on with *"Neither do people light a lamp and put it under a bowl. Instead they put it on its stand, and it gives light to everyone in the house."* Jesus isn't telling us to let our light shine when it is convenient for us, He wants us to always let our light shine.

REFLECTIONS

"

"

GREAT JOY

❝To Him who is able to keep you from falling and to present you before His glorious presence without fault and with great joy—to the only God our Savior be glory, majesty, power and authority, through Jesus Christ our Lord, before all ages, now and forevermore. Amen.**❞**   —Jude 24-25

Think of it, Jesus not only wants to present us before God, He wants to do it with great joy! We cannot imagine the joy and delight God takes in each one of us, His chosen ones. Jude talks about how grand and glorious God's presence is and then Jesus will present us into that glory, with joy. God has been telling us this throughout the Bible. In the Old Testament He tells us in Zephaniah 3:17 *"The Lord your God is with you, He is mighty to save. He will take great delight in you, He will quiet you with His love, He will rejoice over you with singing."* We see God's greatness and how mighty He is but He is such a personal God and takes great joy in you—personally!

Jude 25 tells us how grand and glorious this will all be but then to think of all the people that have gone before us, those here on earth now and all the future generations. We cannot fathom how many souls that can be but God cares for YOU! He is a very personal God and wants all the best for you.

He wants you to reach out to Him, acknowledge your sin and need for a Savior and accept Him as Lord of your life. I am looking forward to seeing my Lord and then to meet all of you in heaven!

REFLECTIONS

"

"

CPSIA information can be obtained at www.ICGtesting.com
Printed in the USA
BVOW11s1816250914

368143BV00011B/207/P